A Gift From:

_____

Date:

_____

A Spoonful of Sugar
For Friends

A Spoonful of Sugar
For Friends

When we hurt each other, we should write it down in the sand, so the winds of forgiveness can make it go away for good. When we help each other, we should chisel it in stone, lest we never forget the love of a friend.
Christian H. Godefroy

Whether it's the best of times or the worst of times, it's the only time we've got.
Art Buchwald

You can make more friends in two months by becoming interested in other people than you can in two years by trying to get other people interested in you.
Dale Carnegie

Am I not destroying my enemies
when I make friends of them?
Abraham Lincoln

An insincere and evil friend is more to be feared
than a wild beast; a wild beast may wound your
body, but an evil friend will wound your mind.
Buddha

Anyone can sympathize with the sufferings of
a friend, but it requires a very fine nature to
sympathize with a friend's success.
Oscar Wilde

Associate yourself with men of good quality
if you esteem your own reputation, for 'tis
better to be alone than in bad company.
George Washington

Be who you are, and say what you feel
because those who mind don't matter,
and those who matter don't mind.
Dr. Seuss

If you put a small value on yourself, rest assured
that the world will not raise your price.
Unknown

The love of our neighbor in all its fullness
simply means being able to say to him,
"What are you going through?"
Simone Weil

But friendship is precious, not only in the shade,
but in the sunshine of life, and thanks to a
benevolent arrangement of things, the
greater part of life is sunshine.
Thomas Jefferson

Celebrate the happiness that friends are always giving;
make every day a holiday and celebrate just living!
Amanda Bradley

Don't be dismayed at good-byes. A farewell
is necessary before you can meet again.
And meeting again, after moments or lifetimes,
is certain for those who are friends.
Richard Bach

Don't flatter yourself that friendship authorizes you to
say disagreeable things to your intimates. The nearer
you come into relation with a person, the more
necessary do tact and courtesy become.
Oliver Wendell Holmes

I have never considered a difference of opinion in
politics, in religion, in philosophy, as a cause for
withdrawing from a friendship.
Thomas Jefferson

Sugar for Friends

I keep my friends as misers do their treasures
because, of all things granted us by wisdom,
none is greater or better than friendship.
Pietro Aretino

If a friend is in trouble, don't annoy him by asking
him if there's anything you can do. Think of
something appropriate and do it.
E. W. Howe

If a man does not make new acquaintances, as he
advances through life, he soon will find himself alone.
A man should keep his friendship in constant repair.
Samuel Johnson

If you hate a person, you hate something in him that is a part of yourself. What isn't part of ourselves doesn't disturb us.
Hermann Hesse Demian

Keep away from people who try to belittle your ambitions. Small people always do that, but the really great ones make you feel that you too can become great.
Mark Twain

A friend is someone who knows the song in your heart and can sing it back to you when you have forgotten the words.
Unknown

What we do for ourselves dies with us. What we do for others and the world remains and is immortal.
Albert Pine

What we have once enjoyed, we can never lose. All that we love deeply becomes a part of us.
Helen Keller

When dealing with people, remember you are not dealing with creatures of logic, but creatures of emotion.
Dale Carnegie

When men and women are able to respect and accept their differences, then love has a chance to blossom.
John Gray

There is an important difference between love and friendship. While the former delights in extremes and opposites, the latter demands equality.
Unknown

The people and circumstances around me do not make me what I am; they reveal who I am.
Dr. Laura Schlessinger

Sugar for Friends

You can't stay in your corner of the forest waiting
for others to come to you; you have to go
to them sometimes.
Winnie the Pooh

It's good to have money and the things that money
can buy, but it's good, too, to make sure you
haven't lost the things that money can't buy.
George Horace Lorimer

It's the little things that matter, that add up in the end,
with the priceless thrilling magic found only in a friend.
Elizabeth Dunphy

Friendship is the source of the greatest pleasures, and without friends, even the most agreeable pursuits become tedious.

St. Thomas Aquinas

Friendship with oneself is all-important because without it one cannot be friends with anyone else in the world.

Eleanor Roosevelt

Grief can take care of itself, but to get the full value of joy, you must have somebody to divide it with.

Mark Twain

We all take different paths in life, but no matter where we go, we take a little of each other everywhere.
Tim McGraw

The world would be so lonely, in sunny hours or gray,
Without the gift of friendship, to help us every day.
Hilda Brett Farr

I cannot even imagine where I would be today were it not for that handful of friends who have given me a heart full of joy. Let's face it:
Friends make life a lot more fun.
Charles R. Swindoll

I have friends in overalls whose friendship I would not swap for the favor of the kings of the world.
Thomas Edison

The truth is that friendship is every bit as sacred and eternal as marriage.
Katherine Mansfield

Friendships that have stood the test
of time and chance are surely best.
Brows may wrinkle, hair grows gray,
Friendship never knows decay.
Unknown

Sugar for Friends

Friendship is almost always the union of a part of one
mind with a part of another; people are friends in spots.
George Santayana

The most called-upon prerequisite
of a friend is an accessible ear.
Maya Angelou

Friendship is the hardest thing in the world to explain.
It's not something you learn in school. But if you
haven't learned the meaning of friendship,
you really haven't learned anything.
Muhammad Ali

"Stay" is a charming word in a friend's vocabulary.
Louisa May Alcott

Did I choose you? Did you choose me? And what difference does it make? All that really matters, friend, is that we chose together.
Lois Wyse

Your friendship is better than chocolate! Well, anyway, it's right up there.
Julie Sutton

It is one of the blessings of old friends that you can afford to be stupid with them.
Ralph Waldo Emerson

Friendship improves happiness and abates misery, by the doubling of our joy and the dividing of our grief.
Marcus Tullius Cicero

Remember, the greatest gift is not found in a store nor under a tree, but in the hearts of true friends.
Cindy Lew

Walking with a friend in the dark is better
than walking alone in the light.
Helen Keller

My friend is not perfect—no more than I am—
and so we suit each other admirably.
Alexander Smith

Say what you mean to do ... and take it for granted
you mean to do right. Never do a wrong thing to
make a friend or keep one. ... You will wrong him
and wrong yourself by equivocation of any kind.
Robert E. Lee

You just don't luck into things as much as you'd like to think you do. You build step by step, whether it's friendships or opportunities.

Barbara Bush

Write down the advice of him who loves you, though you like it not at present.

Italian Proverb

Perhaps the most delightful friendships are those in which there is much agreement, much disputation, and yet more personal liking.

George Eliot

Value friendship for what there is in it, not for what can be gotten out of it.
H. Clay Trumbull

Friends are like melons. Shall I tell you why? To find a good one, you must a hundred try.
Claude Mermet

One friend in a lifetime is much; two are many; three are hardly possible.
Henry Adams

Sugar for Friends

A friend is one who dislikes the
same people you dislike.
Unknown

We should behave to our friends as we
would wish our friends behave to us.
Aristotle

Have friends.
'Tis a second existence.
Baltasar Gracian

Wishing to be friends is quick work, but the most beautiful discovery true friends make is that they can grow separately without growing apart.
Elisabeth Foley

Friends are God's way of apologizing to us for our families.
Unknown

Go often to the house of thy friend, for weeds choke the unused path.
Ralph Waldo Emerson

Friendship is a slow-ripening fruit.
Aristotle

A true friend is someone who thinks that
you are a good egg even though he
knows that you are slightly cracked.
Bernard Meltzer

Are you upset little friend? Have you been lying
awake worrying? Well, don't worry. ... I'm here.
The flood waters will recede, the famine will end,
the sun will shine tomorrow, and I will always
be here to take care of you.
Charlie Brown to Snoopy

You meet people who forget you. You forget people you meet. But sometimes you meet those people you can't forget. Those are your friends.
Unknown

Only a life lived for others is worth living.
Albert Einstein

A friend will tell you she saw your old boyfriend—and he's a priest.
Erma Bombeck

Sugar for Friends

When the character of a man is not
clear to you, look at his friends.
Japanese Proverb

When you choose your friends, don't be short-changed
by choosing personality over character.
W. Somerset Maugham

When you judge another, you do not
define them; you define yourself.
Wayne Dyer

Friendship is a knot tied by angels' hands.
Unknown

Winning has always meant much to me,
but winning friends has meant the most.
Babe Didrikson Zaharias

Without friends, no one would want to live,
even if he had all other goods.
Aristotle

A real friend is one who walks in when
the rest of the world walks out.
Walter Winchell

A single rose can be my garden ...
a single friend, my world.
Leo Buscaglia

The friendship that can cease
has never been real.
Saint Jerom

The hand cannot reach higher
than does the heart.
Orison Swett Marden

Never explain—your friends do not need it, and your
enemies will not believe you anyway.
Elbert Hubbard

Do not protect yourself by a fence,
but rather by your friends.
Czech Proverb

Every man should have a fair-sized cemetery
in which to bury the faults of his friends.
Henry Brooks Adams

Write it on your heart that every day is
the best day of the year.
Ralph Waldo Emerson

Plant a seed of friendship; reap
a bouquet of happiness.
Lois L. Kaufman

Remember that great love and great
achievements involve great risk.
Unknown

All that is worth cherishing begins in
the heart, not the head.
Suzanne Chapin

Reach high, for stars lie hidden in your soul. Dream
deep, for every dream precedes the goal.
Ralph Vaull Starr

Tough times never last, but tough people do.
Robert Schuller

True friendship brings sunshine to the shade,
and shade to the sunshine.
Thomas Burke

Keep your feet on the ground, but let your
heart soar as high as it will.
W. Tozer

Friendship is like a glass ornament; once it is broken, it can rarely be put back together exactly the same way.
Unknown

I would rather have a million friends than a million dollars.
Edward Vernon Rickenbacker

If you look for the worst in people and expect to find it, you surely will.
Abraham Lincoln

If you live to be a hundred, I want to live
to be a hundred minus one day, so I
never have to live without you.
Winnie the Pooh

Kind words can be short and easy to speak,
but their echoes are truly endless.
Mother Teresa

Laughter is the shortest distance
between two people.
Victor Borge

Life without a friend is like death without a witness.
Spanish Proverb

Life's most urgent question is: What
are you doing for others?
Martin Luther King Jr.

A friendship is one soul living in two bodies.
Unknown

What is thine is mine, and all mine is thine.
Titus Maccius Plautus

A friend is a person with whom I may be sincere.
Before him I may think aloud.
Ralph Waldo Emerson

A friend is a present you give yourself.
Robert Louis Stevenson

A friend may well be reckoned the
masterpiece of nature.
Ralph Waldo Emerson

A friend in need is a friend indeed.
Latin Proverb

A good friend remembers what we were
and sees what we can be.
Unknown

No man can be happy without a friend, nor
be sure of his friend till he is unhappy.
Thomas Fuller

No matter how busy you are, you must take time
to make the other person feel important.
Mary Kay Ash

My best friend is the one who
brings out the best in me.
Henry Ford

My friends are my estate.
Emily Dickinson

The language of friendship is
not words but meanings.
Henry David Thoreau

No duty is more urgent
than that of returning thanks.
Unknown

What you risk reveals what you value.
Jeanette Winterson

The love we give away is the only love we keep.
Elbert Hubbard

The most important trip you may take in
life is meeting people halfway.
Henry Boyle

You cannot be friends upon any other terms
than upon the terms of equality.
Woodrow Wilson

You cannot do a kindness too soon, for you
never know how soon it will be too late.
Ralph Waldo Emerson

In a friend you find a second self.
Isabelle Norton

In the sweetness of friendship, let there be
laughter and sharing of pleasures.
Kahlil Gibran

A best friend is better than a guardian angel.
Unknown

Friendship was given by nature to be an assistant
to virtue, not a companion to vice.
Marcus Tullius Cicero

Good friends are good for your health.
Irwin Sarason

Have no friends not equal to yourself.
Confucius

Truth and tears clear the way to a
deep and lasting friendship.
Unknown

Sugar for Friends

Friendship is always a sweet responsibility,
never an opportunity.
Kahlil Gibran

Friendship is like money, easier made than kept.
Samuel Butler

Think twice before burdening a friend with a secret.
Marlene Dietrich

Hold a true friend with both your hands.
Nigerian Proverb

Misfortune tests the sincerity of friends.
Aesop

All love that has not friendship for its base
is like a mansion built upon the sand.
Ella Wheeler Wilcox

Between friends there is no need of justice.
Aristotle

Friendship is a treasured gift, and every time I talk with
you, I feel as if I'm getting richer and richer.
Unknown

If you want people to notice your faults,
start giving advice.
Kelly Stephens

Some people go to priests; others to
poetry; I to my friends.
Virginia Woolf

The best mirror is an old friend.
Peter Nivio Zarlenga

Life is partly what we make it, and partly what it is
made by the friends we choose.
Tennessee Williams

Sugar for Friends

I have learned that to have a good friend is the purest of all God's gifts, for it is a love that has no exchange of payment.
Frances Farmer

A true friend is one who knows all about you and likes you anyway.
Christi Mary Warner

The best kind of friend is the kind you can sit on a porch swing with, never say a word, then walk away feeling like it was the best conversation that you ever had.
Unknown

Sometimes being a friend means mastering the art of timing. There is a time for silence. A time to let go and allow people to hurl themselves into their own destiny. And a time to prepare to pick up the pieces when it's all over.
Gloria Naylor

The only way to have a friend is to be one.
Ralph Waldo Emerson

A true friend never gets in your way unless you happen to be going down.
Arnold H. Glasgow

A true friend is someone who is there for you—
when he'd rather be anywhere else.
Len Wein

One who looks for a friend without
faults will have none.
Hasidic Proverb

You can gain a friend in a year but
lose a friend in a minute.
Unknown

The friend who can be silent with us in a moment of despair or confusion, who can stay with us in an hour of grief and bereavement, who can tolerate not knowing ... not healing, not curing ... that is a friend who cares.

Henri Nouwen

A true friend is the best possession.

Benjamin Franklin

True love is when you have to watch a friend leave, with the knowledge that you might never see him again. But you know he'll be in your mind and heart forever.

Unknown

A true friend knows your weaknesses but shows you your strengths, feels your fears but fortifies your faith, sees your anxieties but frees your spirit, recognizes your disabilities but emphasizes your possibilities.
William Arthur Ward

The comfort of having a friend may be taken away—but not that of having had one.
Seneca

May good luck be your friend in whatever you do, and may trouble be always a stranger to you.
Irish Blessings

The best thing to give to your enemy is forgiveness; to an opponent, tolerance; to a friend, your heart; to your child, a good example; to a father, deference; to your mother, conduct that will make her proud of you; to yourself, respect; to all men, charity.
Benjamin Franklin

True friendship multiplies the good in
life and divides its evils.
Baltasar Gracian

Speak well of your friend; of your enemy say nothing.
Italian Proverb

Time or distance cannot touch the
friendship of the heart.
Unknown

Never cease loving a person, and never give up
hope for him, for even the prodigal son who had
fallen most low could still be saved; the bitterest
enemy and also he who was your friend could again
be your friend; love that has grown cold can kindle.
Soren Kierkegaard

No enemy is so annoying as one who was a friend,
or still is a friend, and there are many more
of these than one would suspect.
William Saroyan

Confidence is the bond of friendship.
Publilius Syrus

True friendship isn't about being there when it's convenient; it's about being there when it's not.
Unknown

The finest kind of friendship is between people who expect a great deal of each other but never ask it.
Sylvia Bremer

One measure of friendship consists not in the number of things friends can discuss, but in the number of things they need no longer mention.
Clifton Paul Fadiman

True friendship comes when the silence between two people is comfortable.
David Tyson Gentry

Love is the only force capable of transforming an enemy into friend.
Martin Luther King Jr.

Among life's precious jewels,
Genuine and rare,
The one that we call friendship
Has worth beyond compare.
Unknown

What do we live for, if it is not to make
life less difficult for each other?
George Eliot

I no doubt deserved my enemies, but I
don't believe I deserved my friends.
Walt Whitman

Friendship may, and often does, grow into love, but love never subsides into friendship.
Lord Byron

Friendship is born at that moment when one person says to another, "What! You, too? I thought I was the only one."
C.S. Lewis

It is only with the heart that one can see rightly; what is essential is invisible to the eye.
Antoine De Saint-Exupery

Depth of friendship does not depend on
length of acquaintance.
Rabindranath Tagore

The real test of friendship is: Can you literally do
nothing with the other person? Can you enjoy those
moments of life that are utterly simple?
Eugene Kennedy

There are not many things in life so beautiful as true
friendship, and not many things more uncommon.
Unknown

58

There is nothing on this earth more to be prized than true friendship.
St. Thomas Aquinas

The royal road to a man's heart is to talk to him about the things he treasures most.
Dale Carnegie

Respect your fellow human being, treat them fairly, disagree with them honestly, enjoy their friendship, explore your thoughts about one another candidly, work together for a common goal, and help one another achieve it.
Bill Bradley

Friendship is the only cement that will
ever hold the world together.
Woodrow T. Wilson

Friendship, like love, is destroyed by long absence,
though it may be increased by short intermissions.
Samuel Johnson

If we would build on a sure foundation in friendship, we
must love friends for their sake rather than for our own.
Charlotte Bronte

People who have a lot of money and no time we call "rich." People who have time but no money we call "poor." Yet the most precious gifts—love, friendship, time with loved ones—grow only in the sweet soil of "unproductive" time.

Unknown

To be capable of steady friendship or lasting love are the two greatest proofs, not only of goodness of heart, but of strength of mind.

William Hazlitt

Expect the dawn of a new beginning in the dark nights of life.

Lloyd John Ogilvie

There is a scarcity of friendship, but not of friends.
Thomas Fuller

Where there are friends, there is wealth.
Titus Muccius Plautus

Friendship is a plant of slow growth and must undergo and withstand the shocks of adversity before it is entitled to the appellation.
George Washington

Laughter is not at all a bad beginning for a friendship,
and it is far the best ending for one.
Oscar Wilde

Much of the vitality in a friendship lies in the honoring of
differences, not simply in the enjoyment of similarities.
Unknown

Never shall I forget the days I spent with you. Continue
to be my friend, as you will always find me yours.
Ludwig van Beethoven

The greatest healing therapy is friendship and love.
Hubert H. Humphrey

It is important to our friends to believe that we are
unreservedly frank with them, and important
to friendship that we are not.
Miguel de Unamuno

Life has no pleasure higher or nobler
than that of friendship.
Samuel Johnson

Sugar for Friends

Friendship is a priceless treasure never to be bought or sold—it can only be cherished.
Unknown

The essence of true friendship is to make allowance for another's little lapses.
David Storey

The best friend will probably acquire the best wife because a good marriage is founded on the talent for friendship.
Friedrich Nietzsche

The most I can do for my friend is simply to be his friend. I have no wealth to bestow on him. If he knows that I am happy in loving him, he will want no other reward. Is not friendship divine in this?

Henry David Thoreau

Be slow to fall into friendship, but when thou art in, continue firm and constant.

Socrates

No love, no friendship can cross the path of our destiny without leaving some mark on it forever.

Francois Muriac

Sugar for Friends

If I can stop one heart from breaking,
I shall not live in vain;
If I can ease one life from aching, or cool one pain,
or help one fainting robin unto his nest again,
I shall not live in vain.
Emily Dickinson

Ultimately the bond of all companionship, whether in
marriage or in friendship, is conversation.
Oscar Wilde

Love is blind, but friendship closes its eyes.
Unknown

Of all the things which wisdom provides to
make life entirely happy, the greatest
is the possession of friendship.
Epicurus

Friendship is a strong and habitual inclination
in two persons to promote the good and
happiness of one another.
Eustace Budgell

Love is flower-like;
Friendship is like a sheltering tree.
Samuel Taylor Coleridge

Life is nothing without friendship.
Marcus Tullius Cicero

The happiest business in all the world
is that of making friends,
And no investment on the street
pays larger dividends,
For life is more than stocks and bonds,
and love than rate percent,
And he who gives in friendship's name
shall reap what he has spent.
Unknown

Friendship flourishes at the fountain of forgiveness.
William Arthur Ward

To let friendship die away by negligence and silence is certainly not wise. It is voluntarily to throw away one of the greatest comforts of the weary pilgrimage.
Samuel Johnson

No distance of place or lapse of time can lessen the friendship of those who are thoroughly persuaded of each other's worth.
Robert Southey

There are no rules for friendship. It must be left to itself. We cannot force it any more than love.
William Hazlitt

Sugar for Friends

Strangers are just friends waiting to happen.
To become a good man, one must have faithful
friends, or outright enemies.
Napoleon

Friendship is the golden thread that ties
the heart of all the world.
Unknown

Friendship makes prosperity brighter, while it lightens
adversity by sharing its griefs and anxieties.
Marcus Tullius Cicero

A tree is known by its fruit; a man by his deeds. A good deed is never lost; he who sows courtesy reaps friendship, and he who plants kindness gathers love.
St. Basil

Friendship is the only cure for hatred,
the only guarantee of peace.
Buddha

It is only the great hearted who can be true friends.
The mean and cowardly can never know
what true friendship means.
Charles Kingsley

True friendship is like sound health; the value
of it is seldom known until it be lost.
Charles Caleb Colton

The highest form of wisdom is kindness.
The Talmud

A friend is very different from an acquaintance.
The former is tried and true; the latter only
a casual shadow in one's life.
Unknown

A good companion shortens the longest road.
Turkish Proverb

Friends are as companions on a journey who ought to aid each other to persevere in the road to a happier life.
Pythagoras

Broken friendships can be soldered, but never sound.
Unknown

The love of our private friends is the only preparatory exercise for the love of all men.

John Henry Newman

One's oldest friend is the best.

Titus Maccius Plautus

A difficult time can be more readily endured if we retain the conviction that our existence holds a purpose—a cause to pursue, a person to love, a goal to achieve.

John Maxwell

Happiness is time spent with a friend and looking foward to sharing time with them again.
Lee Wilkinson

Friendship is never established as an understood relation. It is a miracle which requires constant proofs. It is an exercise of the purest imagination and of the rarest faith.
Henry David Thoreau

Remember, you can earn more money, but when time is spent, it is gone forever.
Zig Ziglar

The art of acceptance is the art of making someone
who has just done you a small favor wish that he might
have done you a greater one.
Martin Luther King Jr.

There can be no friendship without confidence,
and no confidence without integrity.
Unknown

What comes from the heart, goes to the heart.
Samuel Taylor Coleridge

A loving heart is the truest wisdom.
Charles Dickens

Friendship is a living thing that lasts only as long as it is
nourished with kindness, empathy, and understanding.
Unknown

I have made it a rule of my life never to regret
and never to look back. Regret is an appalling
waste of energy. You can't build on it;
it's only good for wallowing in.
Katherine Mansfield

Sugar for Friends

When we seek to discover the best in others, we
somehow bring out the best in ourselves.
William Arthur Ward

Kindness in words creates confidence.
Kindness in thinking creates profoundness.
Kindness in giving creates love.
Lao Tzu

Ah, how good it feels ...
the hand of an old friend.
Mary Englebright

The greatest happiness of life is the conviction
that we are loved—loved for ourselves, or
rather, loved in spite of ourselves.
Victor Hugo

Remember this—very little is needed
to make a happy life.
Marcus Aurelius Antoninus

Anyone with a heart full of friendship
has a hard time finding enemies.
Unknown

Everyone wants to be appreciated, so if you appreciate someone, don't keep it a secret.
Mary Kay Ash

Your vision will become clear only when you can look into your own heart. Who looks outside, dreams; who looks inside, awakens.
Carl Jung

In the middle of difficulty lies opportunity.
Albert Einstein

Life isn't about finding yourself.
Life is about creating yourself.
George Bernard Shaw

It is the heart that makes a man rich. He is rich
according to what he is, not according to what he has.
Henry Ward Beecher

Don't bother just to be better than your contemporaries
or predecessors. Try to be better than yourself.
William Faulkner

Do not say, "It is morning," and dismiss it with a
name of yesterday. See it for the first time
as a newborn child that has no name.
Rabindranath Tagore

Every single one of us can do things that no one else
can do—can love things that no one else can love. We
are like violins. We can be used for doorstops, or we
can make music. You know what to do.
Barbara Sher

I get by with a little help from my firends.
John Lennon

The influence of each human being on others
in this life is a kind of immortality.
John Quincy Adams

Better to light a candle than to curse the darkness.
Chinese Proverb

A light heart lives long.
William Shakespeare

Too late we learn, a man must hold his friend
Unjudged, accepted, trusted to the end.
John Boyle O'Reilly

My best friend is the one who
brings out the best in me.
Henry Ford

People do not attract that which they
want, but that which they are.
James Allen

The best and most beautiful things in the
world cannot be seen or even touched.
They must be felt with the heart.
Helen Keller

Sometimes when I consider what tremendous
consequences come from little things … I am
tempted to think … there are no little things.
Bruce Barton

Our sweetest experiences of affection are meant
to point us to that realm which is the real
and endless home of the heart.
Henry Ward Beecher

To find one real friend in a lifetime is good fortune;
to keep him is a blessing.
Baltasar Gracian

Few cases of eye strain have been developed by
looking on the bright side of things.
Unknown

Go confidently in the direction of your dreams!
Live the life you've imagined.
Henry David Thoreau

It is of practical value to learn to like yourself. Since you must spend so much time with yourself, you might as well get some satisfaction out of the relationship.

Norman Vincent Peale

A kind heart is a fountain of gladness, making everything in its vicinity freshen into smiles.

Washington Irving

The most important single ingredient in the formula of success is knowing how to get along with people.

Theodore Roosevelt

An aim in life is the only fortune worth finding.
Jacqueline Kennedy Onassis

Strange is our situation here upon Earth. Each of us comes for a short visit, not knowing why, yet sometimes seeming to divine a purpose. From the standpoint of daily life, however, there is one thing we do know: that man is here for the sake of other men.
Albert Einstein

If you want to know me, look inside your heart.
Lao Tzu

Now join your hands, and with your hands your hearts.
William Shakespeare

Know that you yourself are a miracle.
Norman Vincent Peale

Don't walk in front of me, I may not follow.
Don't walk behind me, I may not lead.
Walk beside me and be my friend.
Albert Camus

Forever is composed of nows.
Emily Dickinson

Life's problems wouldn't be called "hurdles" if
there wasn't a way to get over them.
Unknown

Use your precious moments to live life fully
every single second of every single day.
Marcia Wieder

A Spoonful of

The heart of a fool is in his mouth, but the mouth of a wise man is in his heart.
Benjamin Franklin

If you view all the things that happen to you, both good and bad, as opportunities, then you operate out of a higher level of consciousness.
Les Brown

Good luck is another name for tenacity of purpose.
Ralph Waldo Emerson

Sugar for Friends

Each person's only hope for improving his lot rests on his recognizing the true nature of his basic personality, surrendering to it, and becoming who he is.

Sheldon Kopp

The best rule of friendship is to keep your heart a little softer than your head.

Unknown

To handle yourself, use your head; to handle others, use your heart.

Eleanor Roosevelt

We talk about the quality of product and service.
What about the quality of our relationships
and the quality of our communications and
the quality of our promises to each other?
Max de Pree

A man is what he thinks about all day long.
Ralph Waldo Emerson

Two may talk together under the same roof
for many years, yet never really meet, and
two others at first speech are old friends.
Mary Catherwood

Every heart that has beat strong and cheerfully
has left a hopeful impulse behind it in the world
and bettered the tradition of mankind.
Robert Louis Stevenson

God has given each of us our "marching orders." Our
purpose here on Earth is to find those orders and carry
them out. Those orders acknowledge our special gifts.
Soren Kierkegaard

I advise you to say your dream is possible
and then overcome all inconveniences, ignore
all the hassles, and take a running leap
through the hoop, even if it is in flames.
Les Brown

Treasure your relationships, not your possessions.
Anthony J D'Angelo

When your true purpose is to help
others succeed, you succeed.
Unknown

The meaning of life is to give life meaning.
Ken Hudgins

Every situation, every moment is of infinite worth;
for it is the representative of a whole eternity.
Johann Wolfgang von Goethe

One learns people through the heart,
not the eyes or the intellect.
Mark Twain

If you can imagine it, you can achieve it.
If you can dream it, you can become it.
William Arthur Ward

Every noble work is at first impossible.
Thomas Carlyle

Be yourself. The world worships the original.
Ingrid Bergman

At the center of your being you have the answer: You
know who you are, and you know what you want.
Lao Tzu

Always be a first-rate version of yourself, instead of a
second-rate version of somebody else.
Judy Garland

Here is a test to find out whether your mission
in life is complete. If you're alive, it isn't.
Richard Bach

Treat people as if they were what they ought to be and
you help them to become what they are capable of being.
Johann Wolfgang von Goethe

Great hearts steadily send forth the secret forces
that incessantly draw great events.
Ralph Waldo Emerson

Find a purpose in life so big it will challenge
every capacity to be at your best.
David O. McKay

Nothing is impossible to a valiant heart.
Jeanne D'Albret

The more you recognize and express gratitude
for the things you have, the more you will
have to express gratitude for.
Zig Ziglar

If you wish your merit to be known,
acknowledge that of other people.
Asian Proverb

He who has a why to live for can bear almost any how.
Friedrich Nietzsche

No love, no friendship, can cross the path of our destiny without leaving some mark on it forever.

Francois Mocuriac

Life's splendor forever lies in wait about each one of us in all its fullness, but veiled from view, deep down, invisible, far off. It is there, though, not hostile, not reluctant, not deaf. If you summon it by the right word, by its right name, it will come.

Franz Kafka

A new friendship is like an unripened fruit—it may become either an orange or a lemon.

Emma Stacey

Getting people to like you is merely
the other side of liking them.
Norman Vincent Peale

Become so wrapped up in something
that you forget to be afraid.
Lady Bird Johnson

If you have built castles in the air, your work
need not be lost; that is where they should be.
Now put the foundations under them.
Henry David Thoreau

Men are motivated and empowered when they feel needed. Women are motivated and empowered when they feel cherished.
John Gray

Few are those who see with their own eyes and feel with their own hearts.
Albert Einstein

All of us have at least one great voice deep inside.
Pat Riley

Give me a lever long enough and a prop strong enough. I can single-handedly move the world.
Archimedes

Enthusiasm, if fueled by inspiration and perseverance, travels with passion, and its destination is excellence.
Napoleon Hill

All the knowledge I possess, everyone can acquire, but my heart is all my own.
Johann Wolfgang von Goethe

Everyone can be great, because everyone can serve.
Martin Luther King Jr.

Have a strong mind and a soft heart.
Anthony J. D'Angelo

If what you're working for really matters,
you'll give it all you've got.
Nido Qubein

Every great achievement is the
victory of a flaming heart.
Ralph Waldo Emerson

If you surrender completely to the moments as they
pass, you live more richly those moments.
Anne Morrow Lindbergh

Few things in the world are more powerful than a
positive push. A smile. A word of optimism and hope. A
"you can do it" when things are tough.
Richard M. DeVos

I count myself in nothing else so happy
As in a soul rememb'ring my good friends.
William Shakespeare

Cherish your visions; cherish your ideals; cherish the
music that stirs in your heart, the beauty that forms in
your mind, the loveliness that drapes your purest
thoughts, for out of them will grow delightful conditions,
all heavenly environment; of these, if you but remain
true to them, your world will at last be built.
James Allen

Be not simply good; be good for something.
Henry David Thoreau

I am here for a purpose and that purpose is to grow into a mountain, not to shrink to a grain of sand. Henceforth will I apply ALL my efforts to become the highest mountain of all, and I will strain my potential until it cries for mercy.
Og Mandino

Look within. Be still. Free from fear and attachment, know the sweet joy of the way.
Buddha

What sunshine is to flowers, smiles are to humanity. They are but trifles, to be sure, but scattered along life's pathway, the good they do is inconceivable.
Unknown

Within your heart, keep one still,
secret spot where dreams may go.
Louise Driscoll

Part of the happiness of life consists not in
fighting battles, but in avoiding them.
A masterly retreat is in itself a victory.
Norman Vincent Peale

Strive to have friends, for life without friends
is like life on a desert island.
Baltasar Gracian

The greatest strength is gentleness.
Iroquois Proverb

Best friends are like diamonds, precious and rare;
False friends are like leaves, found everywhere.
Unknown

The best remedy for those who are afraid, lonely,
or unhappy is to go outside, somewhere where
they can be quiet, alone with the heavens, nature,
and God. Because only then does one feel that
all is as it should be and that God wishes to see
people happy, amidst the simple beauty of nature.
Anne Frank

Love yourself and be awake—
today, tomorrow, always.
Unknown

Wheresoever you go, go with all your heart.
Confucius

True friendship can afford true knowledge. It does not
depend on darkness and ignorance.
Henry David Thoreau

A word of kindness can warm three winter months.
Japanese Proverb

It seems to me that trying to live without friends is
like milking a bear to get cream for your morning
coffee. It is a whole lot of trouble, and
then not worth much after you get it.
Zorah Neale Hurston

A friend is one to whom one may pour out all the
contents of one's heart, chaff and grain together,
knowing that the gentlest of hands will take and sift it,
keep what is worth keeping, and with a breath of
kindness blow the rest away.
Arabic Proverb

Wherever you are, it is your friends
who make the world.
William James

Friends are the family we choose for ourselves.
Edna Buchanan

Remember, we all stumble, every one of us.
That's why it's a comfort to go hand in hand.
Emily Kimbrough

Sugar for Friends

There are two ways of spreading light—to be the candle or the mirror that reflects it.
Edith Wharton

It takes a long time to grow an old friend.
John Leonard

We are all angels with only one wing.
We can only fly while embracing each other.
Luciano de Crescenzo

A good friend knows everything about
you and loves you just the same.
Unknown

One loyal friend is worth ten thousand relatives.
Euripides

When true friends meet in adverse hour;
'Tis like a sunbeam through a shower.
A watery way an instant seen,
The darkly closing clouds between.
Sir Walter Scott